6 John Quincy Adams 1825–29	7 Andrew Jackson 1829–37	8 Martin Van Buren 1837–41	William Henry Harrison 1841	John Tyler 1841–45
16 Abraham Lincoln 1861–65	17 Andrew Johnson 1865–69	18 Ulysses S. Grant 1869–77	19 Rutherford B. Hayes 1877–81	20 James A. Garfield 1881
27 William Howard Taft 1909–13	28 Woodrow Wilson 1913–21	29 Warren G. Harding 1921–23	30 Calvin Coolidge 1923–29	31 Herbert Hoover 1929–33
37 Richard M. Nixon 1969–74	38 Gerald R. Ford 1974–77	39 Jimmy Carter 1977–81	40 Ronald Reagan 1981–89	41 George H. W. Bush 1989–93

THE WHITE HOUSE HAS BEEN THE HOME AND OFFICE TO EVERY PRESIDENT OF THE UNITED STATES SINCE JOHN ADAMS.

Rocco Travels with the Presidents!

Text by **Rocco Smirne** • Illustrated by **John Hutton**

THE WHITE HOUSE *HISTORICAL ASSOCIATION*

Introduction

Every president of the United States travels to places near and far from the White House to attend important events and to meet people across the country and around the world. For more than two hundred years, the presidents have traveled on horses, trains, ships, cars, airplanes, and helicopters. Sometimes, just for fun, they have also used bicycles, golf carts, Segways, and even parachutes!

One day my friend Rocco Smirne told me he wished he could have gone skydiving with President George H. W. Bush! Rocco is six years old, but he already knows much about the White House and the presidents. So I asked Rocco what other kinds of transportation he would like to explore with the presidents, and he created this book for you to enjoy!

Stewart D. McLaurin
President, White House Historical Association

Hi! I'm Rocco.
The presidents live right here at the White House but they have always had to travel too. Let's go with them!

Many, many years ago, there were no cars, so John Adams, the first president to live in the White House, arrived in a horse-drawn carriage.

Saddle up! The presidents rode on horses for many years. I would like to take a ride on horseback with President Abraham Lincoln. It would be a bumpy ride! And it will take longer than riding in a car— and no radio or TV, just the wind in our hair!

After the railroads were built, presidents could travel all over the United States of America.

Long before Warren G. Harding was the president, he wanted to be a railroad engineer. While he was president, he actually took over the controls and drove the train himself on a trip to Alaska!

All aboard! President Franklin D. Roosevelt often rode the train between Washington, D.C., where the White House is, and New York City. I want to go to New York. And it won't take long to get there from Washington, D.C.!

Presidents have used yachts, sailboats, ocean liners, and many different kinds of boats over the years. I think pedal boats are fun!

President Theodore Roosevelt once traveled on a large battleship called the USS *Louisiana* all the way to Panama. That's a country in Central America. I would like to go even farther—all the way to South America!

President William Howard Taft was the first president to have a car at the White House. It was a very large, powerful car called a steamer. He had a driver who liked to go fast!

Today the president travels in a big black car called a limousine. President Ronald Reagan waved from the limousine in the Inauguration Day Parade!

Some presidents have fun cars too! President Lyndon B. Johnson had a special car that he could also drive in the water . . .

. . . President Joe Biden has a fun convertible.
I love sports cars!

Once airplanes were invented, presidents could fly to countries all around the world!

The president flies to many places. I would like to go to France, England, and China on *Air Force One* with President Bill Clinton! Bon Voyage!

The president's car is often ready and waiting when *Air Force One* lands. When President Barack Obama's car was made, it was named "the Beast" because it is indestructible!

Sometimes presidents go to a camp called Camp David for the weekend or a holiday or an important meeting. President Jimmy Carter liked to ride his bicycle there. I like to ride bikes too. Look! No training wheels!

Many presidents drive around Camp David in golf carts. President Dwight D. Eisenhower liked to play golf too! I would like to play golf with him nearby at Gettysburg, Pennsylvania.

There are many ways for the president to travel, but my favorite is the president's own special helicopter. It is called *Marine One*, and it lands right on the backyard of the White House!

I have to go take another trip with the president. See you next time!

About the Author

Rocco Smirne attends elementary school in Fairfax County, Virginia. He loves to travel to new places with his family! His favorite way to travel is by airplane (because he hasn't been in a helicopter yet)! Rocco is also the co-author of *A White House Alphabet*.

About the Illustrator

John Hutton is a professor of art history at Salem College, and the illustrator of a series of children's books published by the White House Historical Association. He lives in Winston Salem, North Carolina.

THE WHITE HOUSE HISTORICAL ASSOCIATION is a nonprofit educational organization, founded in 1961 for the purpose of enhancing the understanding, appreciation, and enjoyment of the Executive Mansion. All proceeds from the sale of the Association's books and products are used to fund the acquisition of historic furnishings and art work for the permanent White House Collection, assist in the preservation of public rooms, and further its educational mission.

BOARD OF DIRECTORS: Frederick J. Ryan Jr., Chairman; John F. W. Rogers, Vice Chairman and Treasurer; James I. McDaniel, Secretary; Stewart D. McLaurin, President

John T. Behrendt, Michael Beschloss, Teresa Carlson, Jean Case, Janet A. Howard, Knight Kiplinger, Martha Joynt Kumar, Anita McBride, Robert M. McGee, Ann Stock, Ben C. Sutton Jr., Tina Tchen, Gregory W. Wendt; LIAISON: Shawn Benge, Deputy Director, Operations Exercising the Delegated Authority of the Director, National Park Service; EX OFFICIO: Lonnie G. Bunch III, Kaywin Feldman, David S. Ferriero, Carla Hayden, Katherine Malone-France

DIRECTORS EMERITI: John H. Dalton, Nancy M. Folger, Elise K. Kirk, Harry G. Robinson III, Gail Berry West

Vice President of Publishing and Executive Editor: Marcia Mallet Anderson; Editorial and Production Director: Lauren McGwin; Senior Editorial and Production Manager: Kristen Hunter Mason; Editorial and Production Manager: Elyse Werling; Editorial Coordinator: Rebecca Durgin Kerr; Consulting Editor: Ann Hofstra Grogg

Copyright © 2021 by the White House Historical Association

All rights reserved under international copyright conventions. No part of this book may be reproduced or utilized in any form or by any means, electronic or mechanical, including photocopying, recording, or by any information storage and retrieval system, without permission in writing from the publisher. Requests for reprint permissions should be addressed to Rights and Reproductions Manager, White House Historical Association, PO Box 27624, Washington D.C. 20038.

10 9 8 7 6 5 4 3 2 1   Library of Congress Control Number: 2021941565   ISBN 978-1-950273-21-8   Printed in Italy